Entrepreneurial Wisdom

Philosophical Thoughts for an Uncluttered Life

Renn Zaphiropoulos

iUniverse, Inc.
New York   Bloomington

iUniverse books may be ordered through booksellers or by contacting:

iUniverse
1663 Liberty Drive
Bloomington, IN 47403
www.iuniverse.com
1-800-Authors (1-800-288-4677)

Because of the dynamic nature of the Internet, any Web addresses or links
contained in this book may have changed since publication and may no longer be
valid. The views expressed in this work are solely those of the author and do not
necessarily reflect the views of the publisher, and the publisher hereby disclaims
any responsibility for them.

ISBN: 978-1-4401-8299-0 (sc)
ISBN: 978-1-4401-8300-3 (dj)
ISBN: 978-1-4401-8301-0 (ebook)

Printed in the United States of America

iUniverse rev. date: 6/10/10

Dedication

This book is dedicated to the memory of Russell Varian and Alan Watts. I was fortunate to have known them. They were my inspiration to learn very profound truths about management and life itself.

"Years of successful experience in the business and consulting industries have made Renn Zaphiropoulos one of the world's leading thinkers when it comes to applying lessons of leadership to everyday management. More than anything, Renn understands human nature and the importance of valuing human capital above all else. I have found myself applying principles outlined in this book to my role as leader and administrator on a daily basis."

Michael T. Benson
President Southern Utah University

Not only Renn Zaphiropoulos has been a very successful business man (which gives him credibility when he writes about the field) but he has also been a pioneer in the leadership field.

Renn was very well known for his ability to create the proper environment so that people could use their talents and be at their best on the job and, even better, experience what we call today a "mind expansion opportunity". To work with him or just watch him lead was to learn and grow. He was a model of "Creative leadership" (See the video "One day with Renn Zaphiropoulos" designed and created by Professor John Kotter from the Harvard Business School)

Their success was Renn's success! He was able to empower people before the concept was even around. On top of that leadership talent, Renn has (still today) that very special ability to put things into perspective when exploring a leadership situation. He has what so many leaders miss i.e. leadership wisdom! To listen to him is a source of enlightenment and...joy. He makes you think. He challenges you with new perspectives. He makes things that appear at first very complex easy to grasp and use. He is inspiring and at the same time very pragmatic. What a good mix for a leader!

He is a philosopher and a poet. He is what a genuine leader should be...

Professor Pierre Casse
Dean of Berlin School of Creative Leadership

Table of Contents

Introduction

After high school, university, and an industrial experience of fifty three years in the high-tech world, I have gathered a variety of philosophical thoughts by reading, listening to others, and direct personal experience.

The attached list is a distillation of many things I have heard and derived by being a participant in the wonderful world of technology and management. They are expressions of my understanding of life in general, as it manifests itself in organizational behavior and the development of effective human relationships. The emphasis is on developing an attitude that accomplishes the maximum result with the least amount of effort, removes unnecessary clutter, and results in an elegant existence.

The statements are not listed in any particular order, because each on can stand on its own merit. Much of the content has been part of numerous presentations that were given and discussed during my seminars and lectures for the past several years.

If the process of learning can be improved by reading familiar ideas which are expressed in a novel way, then the reader can choose to harvest his or her own benefits by reading this book.

Prologue

I doubt this book will become very popular. The reason for this is that it will not satisfy most people's needs for definite answers to the complicated problems involved in running an enterprise in entrepreneurial management. Unfortunately, there are many books published which seem to indicate that success depends on following a set of instructions, usually mentioned in numbers such as 3, 7, 10, and so on.

In my experience, those who are interested in winning the game, have to understand that there is not enough information to be able to give specific instructions to people for success. Situations change, the requirements become variable and the best that one can hope for is to develop a judgment as to how to change direction when the environment calls for it. Wisdom is not easily obtained and the statement by our parents "you can do anything if you try hard enough" applies only to situations where we have infinite time. We are all faulty and our success depends on being intelligent enough to fail when it doesn't matter. This means we have a responsibility to develop enough knowledge about what we are doing and to define the critical path that depends on establishing a set of priorities.

Most of us who are brought up under the Judeo/ Christian ethic, develop an idea that the world is polarized and that extreme opposites can occur unilaterally, one without the other. During my formative years when I had the great luck and privilege to meet Alan Watts, I finally understood that all opposites are inseparable and we cannot have one without the other. This is why I have adopted the "Zen" point of view and become more realistic as it pertains to my expectations of myself and other people. I finally understood that to succeed Is the other side of failure and no matter how good I am, success will always contain some failure and failure will always contain some success. There is a way of successfully negotiating opposites so a person is not driven obsessively by unrealistic ambitions to become only successful and banish failure forever.

This philosophy is extremely helpful when one tackles difficult situations that contain a lot of risk and where decisions have to be made without complete and rigorous knowledge. The statements that follow this prologue are the result of many years of working and building in the high tech industry. I have finally understood that my success is not measured by how much money I made, but how I did it. It also contains a very serious requirement that to be truly successful, one has to accomplish considerable personal growth by transcending one's conditioning. All the wonderful instructions and principles we learned in our formative years will have to be modified and polished when we become older. It is not that tradition and early value systems are wrong. One has to realize that they had a period of application that was acceptable but in reality they became anachronistic later in life. It is as if we spend a lot of effort learning things that we later have to unlearn. Most psychoanalysts have delved extensively into the effects of early conditioning and the resulting neurotic behavior. We have a responsibility to grow up and stop looking at the world through our adolescent eyes.

Most failures that I have seen in management are the result of very well trained people who refuse to update their ideas and understand that it is preferable to first find the grain of a situation and then go with it. It is not necessary to succeed by becoming some sort of martyr. Success is being a person who is able to abandon ideas that don't work anymore. What a wonderful way to finally come to realize that life should be a process of continuous discovery and that it is okay to occasionally change our mind and put something in it that is new and exciting. One has to acquire self-confidence and not be afraid to change behavior. We don't have to accomplish in order to achieve success. The only requirement is that we become intelligent about our situation and never try to do things that don't make sense. The Zen proverb, "If you want to drown, don't torture yourself in shallow water." makes sense and should be a fundamental principle guiding modern entrepreneurs.

I hope that you enjoy reading the philosophical tidbits that I have gathered through my years of intense management. They are only manifestations of some fundamental that I have found to be true and that still require the judgment of the reader before they are applied. It is an invitation to exercise one's precious processor and act intelligently no matter how difficult the situation may be, to identify the fundamentals involved in solving any problem and not try to violate the fundamental principles. I am sure that anyone reading this book will not become an instantaneous sage; at best it will improve the reader's judgment and awareness and maybe be of some substantial help in recognizing difficult situations and take appropriate action for success.

Business Strategy

A game is any human activity, governed by prescribed rules. You have rules, you have a game. No rules, no game. It can be frivolous or lethal.

■ ■ ■ ■

A human activity that is organized always has a beginning, a middle, and an end. This is usually what we call "the plot." To describe it, one can mention in detail that activity involved. But, it is much more useful to describe the situation by identifying the plot and, therefore, recognize the sequence of events as it pertains to winning or losing it.

You win a game, not because you tried, but because you chose the right game.

■ ■ ■ ■

We are conditioned to try to succeed. It is as if we can succeed at anything. This is an illusion. We are all very different people with different abilities and personalities. It is wise before we start a game to know that it suits us. Not every game is one that we can win almost effortlessly. As we mature, we should forget earlier pressures to be this or that, and discover for ourselves activities and environments in which we can succeed with the least amount of effort.

You cannot win a game if you do not know what it is.

■ ■ ■ ■

It is amazing to me how many people start playing a game without first identifying the rules. Companies do this when they decide to buy a company in order to diversify a market or a product line without thinking the process through and understanding the real requirements after the acquisition occurred. So many times the changes in culture can kill the merger. It is very important to have a post-merger plan in order to understand in advance what the new rules are and how to win the game.

A business is the process of satisfying a human need at a profit.

■■■■

This implies that as a CEO one should be an amateur sociologist. After one identifies the need to be satisfied, one has to be concerned the need will persist in the future. Many needs tend to disappear and if that happens, the company will be in trouble. One should continuously be aware as to what is happening to the need to be satisfied. It is important to understand that the only reason for being a business is to show a profit. Success is presenting a reasonable return to the shareholders that have placed their faith in our ability to manage. To satisfy a need and not make money is called philanthropy. A person who does not satisfy a need, but makes a profit is a crook.

In a free-enterprise system, if you succeed in business, you attract competition that will attempt to take that business away from you. If you do not like the competition, you should plan to fail. No one competes with a failure.

■ ■ ■ ■

Healthy competition is the cause for striving for excellence in business with a customer being the usual beneficiary.

You never start a business unless circumstances are stacked in your favor. You should make sure the need you satisfy persists, and you should continue developing a clear edge over competition.

■ ■ ■ ■

You don't start a business to find out what is going to happen. One minimizes a negative risk by calculating in advance the reason for succeeding. This edge over competition should be articulated and defined as clearly as possible. The need we satisfy and the edge over competition are variable. I suggest that a well-managed company periodically review the situation to make sure that they are unpleasantly surprised by a negative change.

In sport, the difference between competitors is minimized so the result is unpredictable. The fun is guessing the outcome. Business is not sport.

■ ■ ■ ■

We have been conditioned by the phrase, "It doesn't make any difference if you win or lose, but how you play the game." Although this is a noble sentiment, because it insinuates that we should place value on the "way we play," it should be outgrown when we are in business. In order to raise money for an enterprise, the prospective investors should be told how the game will be won. They insist in knowing clearly the edge over competition.

If you want to make a lot of money, you have to discover a latent, unexploited need to satisfy.

■■■■

The above is true because when one discovers something totally new, the competition is absent. An excellent example of this is the invention of the hand-held calculator. Before its introduction, very few people had calculators because they were mechanical, clumsy and expensive. Now I don't know of anyone who doesn't have a calculator. Discovering a latent need presents an opportunity to make a lot of money before the competition arrives on the scene.

Don't try to make a business out of a hobby.

■ ■ ■ ■

When we have a hobby, we get involved with a pleasant activity which has no time limit before the result is obtained. It is not something that is done efficiently and the emphasis is not finishing it. One cannot charge enough money to pay for the time spent.

Making a lot of money involves extraordinary performance.

■ ■ ■ ■

If you set out to start an enterprise to become rich, you should understand that you have to be better than most people and thus plan to be extraordinary. Ordinary behavior commands ordinary reward. In order to get something above the average, you have to perform in a unique and preferable manner.

A vision is a wish with an articulated way of achieving it. A wish is worthless. A vision is what a leader presents to prospective followers.

■ ■ ■ ■

It is amazing to me how many companies start new projects or buy other companies by expressing a wish by the Corporate Development Department. Responsible managers always describe an articulated path to success before entering a new situation. Smart followers will join a leader who has an ability to explain clearly the path to success.

Success

Success depends on reducing the clutter in your life.

■ ■ ■ ■

When we are young, we are told many things which turn out not to be true. Most traditions in life have to be outgrown. The idea is to update oneself and attempt to solve life's problems in an ever-changing and updated way. Failure to do this prolongs the existence of feelings, principles, and expectations that are clutter and reduce the joy of life. We should try not to do the impossible and believe in illusions.

Success occurs when the actual performance divided by the expected is larger than one.

■■■■

The inequality governs the world. Success is synonymous to overachievement. This is why most companies are cautious about developing high expectations of performance. If the company's performance is better than its plan, their stock goes up; if it is less than its plan, their stock goes down.

A stated expectation always precedes an evaluation.

■ ■ ■ ■

We cannot evaluate anything unless we previously state an expectation that we use a ruler. In ethical matters, the expectation is set by the Ten Commandments that cannot be challenged. In business that expectation is man-made and in many situations it can be the part that is wrong.

On evaluating your performance, do not compare yourself to a celebrity. Compare yourself to your own relatives.

■ ■ ■ ■

Over-achieving usually depends on a very particular situation that one finds oneself in. Many people encounter unforeseen, fortuitous circumstances. That's why one should compare one's performance using familiar scenarios that surround one's family and friends.

Failure is the other side of success. Success and failure coexist.

■ ■ ■ ■

This principle, if understood clearly, can prevent someone from feeling devastated when a failure occurs. There is no question that we don't like failure and it should be avoided at all cost. At the same, we should understand that it co-exists with success and it should be expected.

There are too many recipes and not enough good cooks.

■ ■ ■ ■

The secret to good cooking is the way the materials are heated and not necessarily their measurement. What most people do not understand is that a written recipe will not guarantee success. Great cooking depends on the ability to change the heating of materials in an appropriate manner. That requires a great deal of judgment which is obtained through long and frequent practice.

Success does not depend on following instructions. It depends on acquiring a judgment on how to change your direction when the outside world indicates you should.

■ ■ ■ ■

There isn't enough information available to predict exactly what one should do to achieve a desired result. This is where experience comes in. It is the force that can adjust one's behavior to suit the requirements of the outside world.

Most people with "Straight A's" never get over it.

■■■■

When we are young, the longer we study, the better grades we get. If we reject the rest of life and only study with passion, the system rewards us with high marks. The fact is, we become such specialists and very proficient at one subject by neglecting to understand that the rest of life. For example, we may know all about physics or engineering but we can be ignorant when it comes to human relationships, art, literature, sport, food, etc. We get an idea that if we spend a lot of time doing something it will always be better—until we go into business and we find out we have to pay someone to do it. If it takes long, it costs too much money and we make less profit.

Success is not only making money, but how you make it.

■ ■ ■ ■

Money is the report card of our marketability. In many ways it is also a measure of our fairness, honesty and compassion. Being rich is having a lot of money. Being wealthy is being able to spend it joyfully and with a happy heart. Money made the wrong way makes us rich but not wealthy. We should not lose our basic principles just to put some money in the bank.

You may try to succeed with all your might, but it is only worthwhile if the attempt is floated on top of an idea that it really does not make any difference.

■ ■ ■ ■

Success is desirable but it should not be pursued obsessively. We should not take the games we play too seriously. It spoils the fun. On the tennis court we can try to win by being an enemy, but we should do it with the perspective that we are friends. This does not mean that we do not try to win passionately. It only gives us the chance to understand the process intelligently and negotiate successfully the two opposites: winning and losing.

**People who succeed beyond
their wildest dreams lose their
humility and consider themselves
as competent instead of lucky.**

■ ■ ■ ■

*It is always very pleasant to brag about an unexpected and overwhelming
successs. One should not forget that if the actual results are much more
than expected, the event is called an accident. One should never brag
about the hole-in-one.*

To achieve great success you have to be competent enough to capitalize on unforeseen fortuitous circumstances.

■ ■ ■ ■

An overwhelming success involves the process of capitalizing on lucky circumstances. Many people can let opportunity go by without exploiting it because they are not smart enough to capture it. Becoming very successful involves being very aware of the opportunities around us and thus being able to ride a strong wave.

Being very successful is being wrong on the right side.

■ ■ ■ ■

If the actual is much better than the expected you have obviously been wrong in forecasting. The saving grace is that things turned out much better than planned so the error was on the right side. It could have just as easily been on the other side.

Knowing your numbers is important. But success depends upon knowing the plot.

■ ■ ■ ■

In observing and reporting a company's performance, one should never be too detailed and lost in a multitude of numbers. What is important is to understand the trends and develop ideas in how to change direction if necessary. The company should have a defined process that describes its life from the beginning to the middle, and on to the end. One should know the plot.

A group's success usually depends on the prompt exploitation of enthusiasm and the pressure of group champions.

■ ■ ■ ■

Never be afraid to give the job to those who are passionate about getting it. I am sure there are extenuating circumstances when this should not be done, particularly if you are dealing with enthusiastic idiots. Success is usually caused by people who want to change things and are enthusiastic about achieving higher and better results. Whenever possible this enthusiasm should be exploited promptly.

Success is finishing everything with the least amount of effort without decreasing its quality.

■ ■ ■ ■

This is another definition for efficiency. It is a matter of comparing the effort expended to the results obtained. If one does things faster, it does not mean that they are done poorly. It really means that the person is an expert and not an amateur. An amateur will take much longer to do a job, which will cost more and probably be less desirable.

Personal Behavior

If a subordinate leaves your office feeling bad after a meeting, the chances are, you have failed.

■ ■ ■ ■

Assuming that you want a subordinate to continue reporting to you, your objective should be that you inspire the worker to correct his or her behavior rather than feel guilty about it. A typical moralist is a person who insists that the subordinate repents openly and shows regret about their mistakes. The idea of criticizing people should have a positive objective in mind. The person should understand the wrong they have done and then seek your help about becoming better and not failing again. This requires a great deal of understanding and wisdom.

Never own a private parking space unless you are physically challenged.

■ ■ ■ ■

Having a private parking space is a hollow status symbol. No supervisor should obtain an authority status, by seeing his or her name printed on the asphalt. I have been told that this may inspire others to have their name printed on the asphalt very close to the front door. I do not agree. The person who comes in early and has to park in the regular parking lot hates you for having reserved a front-door parking space just because you are a higher rank.

Always make your expectations clear.

■ ■ ■ ■

It is unfortunate that part of our conditioning makes us hesitant in expressing our expectations from others in a forthright manner. The idea is not to be demanding and strong regarding what you want from other people. The fact is, if one makes expectations clear in a non-threatening way, one gives a chance for the subordinate to understand what the environment expects and, therefore, have a chance to act in an appropriate manner. Too many people get fired without knowing why, and expressing surprise that what was expected of them was not really made clear.

It's not lonely upstairs...
unless you close your door.

■■■■

There are those who, when they become a supervisor, feel they suddenly belong to a different class. They start to deal with subordinates at arm's length and they occupy luxurious offices that tend to intimidate any visitor. Their heart and their door are not open. They do not encourage communication. Ironically, they complain that it is lonely upstairs, when they are the one who closed the door.

Don't complain. You have what you want.

■■■■

Most of the time, complaining about one's situation is synonymous to seeking pity from those around you and indulging in talking about one's problems without proposing a solution. Many people complain continuously about a situation they say they do not want, when they refuse to do anything about it. It is as if they get a great deal of satisfaction out of being in an adverse situation rather than terminating it.

The greatest things in this world—love, affection, loyalty, respect, laughter, teamwork, etc.—are not the result of a command. They require cultivation.

■ ■ ■ ■

Successful leaders are conditioned to obtain results by being able to command subordinates. Because they are the boss, they make the mistake of thinking everything in life can be given to them. This is an illusion. Certain feelings and activities desired from others are not subject to command. They can only be the result of cultivating an effective and well-functioning relationship that requires wisdom and patience.

Getting old is not an achievement; getting old is inevitable.

■ ■ ■ ■

Living to a healthy ripe old age depends on being born with the right genes and then not abusing your body. If you want to brag about being old, talk about the quality of the journey rather than its length. Getting old and looking back and feeling it was a great trip with lots of excitement, ups and downs, and acquiring wisdom is something to feel good about.

I want to have all things I don't need. If I have only what I need, then I merely survive.

■■■■

We are conditioned to justify our actions because they satisfy some sort of legitimate and approved need for survival. I believe that after we guarantee survival, what we wish for are the kinds of things that create the "jazz" of life. The reason we buy "this" or "that," is because we like it and it makes us feel good. None of it is really necessary.

I expect pleasant surprises from my subordinates.

■ ■ ■ ■

If I get from my subordinates what I ask for, they merely obey me but do not contribute anything on their own to make the results even better. An inspired subordinate will try to over-achieve and amplify the requested performance. If I ask you to give me a glass of water, you can do just that, or you can put some ice in it and a squeeze of lime. I want to get the lime without giving the order.

As a manager, you are a talent arranger.

■ ■ ■ ■

Human talent can be used like paints on canvas. When the world admires a successful painting it is because of a successful arrangement of colors by the artist. Certain colors look good next to each other—the same applies to people. As a manager, you have the responsibility of arranging the composition so that the desired result is obtained by the organization.

When the organization fails, the people themselves do not fail, the original arrangement is erroneous. (The notes are not wrong, the score is.)

As a manager, you are a human gardener. You help people grow.

■ ■ ■ ■

People can be treated like plants. In order for plants to grow, the gardener must first understand its needs and then make sure the needs are satisfied. This will help the plant grow well and deliver the desired flowers or fruit. People likewise exhibit individual needs and a wise manager will make every attempt to satisfy them. If this is done well, the person is in a flourishing environment and will thrive and exceed expectations. The opposite is also true. When a person is in a frustrating environment, they perform unsatisfactorily. As a manager you can get a reward by hearing someone say, "You have helped me grow to be a better person."

Talking is like cooking; it should never be overdone.

■ ■ ■ ■

We are conditioned to feel that communication is very important between people. But, like everything else, the amount of talking—and particularly the detail involved in talking—should be moderated and not overdone. Too much talking gets in the way of listening to them and paying attention to them.

If you want to be a Communist, the best place to live is China or Cuba.

■ ■ ■ ■

Assuming that you don't want to be a crusader and suffer all the pain associated with crusading, you should live in harmony with the system that is present in your own country. Most of the time it is pointless to try to upset a situation that is not degenerate and that seems to satisfy the wishes of most of the people. You should avoid becoming a crusader in order to attract attention. There are people who constantly go from one crusade to the other because it builds up their self-esteem and makes them feel unique, just because they ally themselves with some extraordinary cause.

Most people are neither liberal nor conservative, but a combination of both.

■ ■ ■ ■

I find it difficult to put myself in either category. There are times when I feel that people are somewhat victims of external circumstances. But most people should do something about it and grow out of the situation rather than wallowing in self-pity. This attitude does not inspire others to take responsibility for their situation by always attributing their failure to others, or the system under which they live. Conversely, people who are full of moralistic views and dogmatic principles tend to make their offspring seek success and morality in an obsessive manner. They may achieve and over-achieve the expected results, but they suffer simultaneously with a great deal of torment because they feel they are required to do so.

A great samurai kills the enemy with one blow. Two blows are in bad taste.

■ ■ ■ ■

There are times when one should make a crisp decision when faced with an unpleasant prospect. Most often the pain of executing an unpleasant task increases when a person hesitates. A great Zen statement is: "If you sit, sit. If you stand, stand. But don't wobble."

When I was young, I did not have enough money to eat well. When I made money, they put me on a diet.

■ ■ ■ ■

A friend of mine used to tell me, "Do not try to win in life, it will always elude you." When you become very wise, you die. It is nature's way of resetting the clock and avoiding anything being done in excess.

Become a person who always honors agreements.

■ ■ ■ ■

This was one of my father's commandments. There is always a reason not to honor an agreement. When we justify a failure, we seem to get solace by believing that it was inevitable and out of our own hands. When we always act with the purpose of keeping our word we develop a reputation of being a person who is dependable. Being dependable and indispensable is the key to job security.

The bigger the size of the desk, the smaller the man behind it.

■■■■

The impressive size and luxury of a desk does not add value and competence of the person that sits behind it. There are companies who have policy manuals that specify the material the desk is made of, according to the rank of the supervisor. This is really an illusion. A man's intelligence does not improve with the size of his chair or the thickness of the carpet in the office.

In our life we always have to choose between two co-existing opposites.

■ ■ ■ ■

Because the principles espoused by the Judeo-Christian ethic, we are conditioned to be polarized regarding opposites such as good and evil, love and hate, etc. After studying the Far Eastern thought, I have come to understand that these things cannot exist unilaterally, i.e. we cannot have one without the other. We know love in terms of hate, hot/cold, success/ failure, etc. Our expectation should not be to banish the negative, but actually reduce it.

Cleaning house is moving dirt from one place to another.

■ ■ ■ ■

Sometimes we feel that when we clean something we have banished the dirt. This applies to our wish to banish anything that we do not like. In reality, that is impossible. I am not suggesting that we learn to like our dirt, what I am saying is that dirt is ubiquitous and it can only be reduced, not eliminated. To try and eliminate it is the equivalent to introducing unnecessary clutter into one's life.

A great fit is better than a larger size.

■ ■ ■ ■

Most of us are conditioned to think that larger is better or that more is better and we miss the fact that something acquires quality and value if it fits an external requirement. A proper measure of anything should be a manifestation of how adequately it fulfills a previously stated expectation.

Most mergers fail because of a clash of human cultures.

■ ■ ■ ■

Mergers and acquisitions are usually initiated by investors, directors, and top management. Most of the time, the concern revolves around complementary markets, products and financial needs. What is missed is that everything will be accomplished by "people," and their ability to perform well depends on their respective cultures. Achieving results is an expression of human needs and they cannot be thought of independently. One has to consider styles of management, geographical location, and personnel policies that govern appropriate reward systems. Failure to do that can result in utter disaster.

Personal growth is transcending one's conditioning.

■ ■ ■ ■

We are all subject to tradition. Most traditions should be used as a bar of soap or a small boat. After we use them, we leave them behind. When we are young we are told many things which do not apply in the latter years of life. They are useful when we are young, and may have prevented us from an untimely death before we turned twenty. But, like the old idea of Santa Claus, they have understood for what they were and transcended when we grow up. This is very difficult to do and it rarely happens successfully because we tend to maintain those beliefs which are comfortable to us. We tend to be afraid of adopting new things, even if they might present an excellent solution to our current problems.

Give the job to the person with the most scars.

■■■■

Except for pathological cases, most people learn from failing. This is what eventually makes the baby able to walk. A human being can learn not only "what to do," but "what not to do." People's experience with past failure can be extremely valuable for future success.

The difficulty about becoming an authority is that one spends his first 25 years as a subordinate.

■ ■ ■ ■

We are born in somebody else's house and our parents tell us what the law is, the policies to follow, and even the IRS determines that we are dependant. We finally leave our house and enter a school where the teacher tells us what the policies are. Later we enter a university and the professors determine what we should do. And, then we get a job and we continue to be subordinate. So far we have succeeded by asking permission, obeying the law, and doing what is expected of us. As a subordinate we are "one of a lower order." That miraculous day when we get the promotion, we are suddenly supposed to become an "authority." This is virtually impossible and most of us have great difficulty in assuming the new role.

If you have a big heart, the whole world comes in.

■■■■

It is a great quality to be unafraid to get close to people and be able to communicate openly and in a forthright manner. Suspicious people always have difficulty in communicating and they usually complain that the world is against them.

When you grow up you make your own ten commandments.

■ ■ ■ ■

In infancy we are told that it is God's word that we should be moral, good, and the like. Depending on one's religion or philosophical bent, we are given a set of rules of conduct if we want to be a good person. When we grow up we find out that these rules are not sufficient and can be subject to a great deal of interpretation to suit one's wishes. We begin to understand that being good should not be the result of obeying any external authority, but it should be our understanding that good behavior is preferable because "it works with people." Morality is then followed as a practical matter and not as obedience to an external communication.

If you satisfy the needs of a lemon tree, the fruit will fall into your hand, without giving it an order.

■ ■ ■ ■

Most people who have achieved authority forget the incredible power of motivation. All we have to do is look at the world around us and see how we can achieve everything we want, by going with nature rather than against it. This is the effortless way. Instead of being forceful and acting as a ruler, we set up an environment under which people flourish naturally.

I envy my dogs. They do not describe, do not rationalize, and don't have the need to judge.

■ ■ ■ ■

Sometimes when I'm anxious and worry about things that don't matter, I look at my sleeping dogs on the carpet and I envy them. It is amazing how much stress we impose on ourselves by trying to do the impossible and satisfy the anachronistic expectation. Our analysis of the world around us, if taken too seriously, if taken too seriously, will get in the way and we can trip ourselves.

Life should be a process of discovery.

■ ■ ■ ■

Although it is pleasant and comfortable to repeat something we know, as a jam session, it does not contribute to growth and the use of our marvelous brain processor. Having succeeded in life by solving a multitude of problems, we get anxious about the ability of our children to do the same. We try to remove any stress by telling them what life's plot is. We, thus, remove the opportunity for them to discover it anew. It's like our coming out of the movie theatre and telling the end of the story to someone who is walking in. We don't realize that purpose for participating in the movie is to enjoy the stress of not knowing how it will end. In this case, being cautious is being destructive. We should let our children experience life using their own brains and thus develop that priceless knowledge by discovering rather than following instructions.

People are motivated to join a team when the process improves their image to themselves.

■ ■ ■ ■

It is amazing how authoritarians reverse a situation and blame someone for not being a team member. What they don't understand is the reason why the person is not a team member is because he or she does not respect their boss. Most people want to be proud of the team they have joined. This is why we have Rolls Royce and Porsche clubs but no clubs of blue Chevys with black tires. It is the responsibility of the leader to attract prospective team members.

A person under constant criticism will eventually lose confidence, psychologically break down, or leave the situation.

■ ■ ■ ■

No one can survive without the support of the environment. Sooner or later we need to hear someone say we are okay. The problem with most managers is they experience criticism as a subordinate and they feel that being critical of others is an essential duty of a supervisor. This is why when we have a meeting we usually "beat up" the person who has not met his plan. We constantly emphasize criticism and dwell in failure. We should realize that although criticism is an essential part of management, it should be done in a way that mobilizes toward corrective action rather than the generation of guilt that is an immobilizing force. It should always be balanced with appropriate positive praise and inspiration.

To optimize performance, a person needs a specific environment in which to flourish.

■ ■ ■ ■

On the outside we are all very much the same but inside we are very different spiritually and culturally. Our needs vary extensively, particularly when it comes to personal attitudes such as ambition, cautiousness, drive, etc. A person's performance depends on how one reacts to an environment. Ideally, one should live in a custom-made environment. This is not always possible. We should always remember that an environment that is not conducive to a person's growth results in diminished performance.

Any rewards, to be meaningful and motivating, have to be perceived as deserved, timely, and followed by a prompt celebration.

■ ■ ■ ■

Designing appropriate incentive plans is an art form that requires a great deal of wisdom. In a successful situation the rewards are most meaningful after they have been hard won. What management often misses is how important it is to be prompt with the delivery. We usually hear excuses that the bonus checks are not ready because the finance department had a lot of work at year's end. This is a false excuse and should be avoided. When an employee is told of a particular bonus, the check should be ready "at that time." The bonus should be followed by a prompt celebration. The celebration should be appropriate according to the size of the reward and always be done in good taste. It is discouraging and diminishes the value of the reward when the check is sent impersonally by mail.

Authority should rule by competence and not by awe. (Erich Fromm)

■■■■

When we are young the authority is fearsome, even if he or she doesn't want to be. Our parents, the priest, the rabbi, the policeman, are always bigger and more powerful. We grow in thinking that fear is a motivator and it is what makes people obey. Nothing could be further from the truth. It is unfortunate that authoritarians continue this by establishing themselves in intimidating office quarters. When one enters the executive row of the Chairman's and President's offices, the rugs get deeper, the paintings more expensive, the lights are soft, and everybody whispers. One gets a feeling this is the real inner sanctum and one better watch out and behave in an acceptable manner or else!

A person has the right to know the significance of what he is doing.

■ ■ ■ ■

There is no question that the job is always done better when the person who is doing it understands the meaning. When I worked at Varian, there was a great deal of effort expended to make sure the workers knew how important their job was. It was a very motivating environment for excellent work. It takes effort from top management to establish this situation.

Most often an apology serves only the person who has acted erroneously.

■ ■ ■ ■

We live in a culture in which when one says, "I'm sorry," is absolved of the crime he or she has committed. The idea of an "ever merciful God," does not really apply. There has to be a distinction between right and wrong and one's attitude toward it. An authority should always act in a way that it is not necessary to apologize for anything. The apology does not benefit any victim. This is why when one becomes an authority; one cannot rely on repentance for approval.

"Class" is when you can behave appropriately in any culture and at any level.

■ ■ ■ ■

To be classy is not limited to acting politely in a palace. It is having enough wisdom and experience to act appropriately at the opposite side of the spectrum. One should be acceptable and act in a correct manner in any milieu.

The most usually practiced form of self-defense is self-deception.

■ ■ ■ ■

Lying to oneself to preserve one's dignity and self-esteem is not a sin, it is self-defense. There is a huge difference in a lie which is fraudulent and one that helps the person preserve his or her dignity. This kind of apparent dishonesty should never be exposed because it removes that last attempt for self-preservation.

The wisdom of knowing that you have been lucky avoids the usual disaster when you try to win again.

■ ■ ■ ■

A person should understand the cause for his or her success. Sometimes it is the result of the simultaneous occurrence of extraordinary fortuitous circumstances. This is where wisdom is very precious because it avoids the pitfall of losing one's humility and trying to win again under different circumstances. Winning or losing does not stand by itself. It is the result of a fit between what is required at a particular time and one's ability to fulfill it. This always varies with a changing environment.

Never be late to a meeting. It shows contempt for those who came on time.

■ ■ ■ ■

When we were young, the authority figure exhibited an apparent arbitrary behavior. This is when orders are given and attitudes prevail which don't have to be justified. The boss acts because he is the boss. He can be late and no one challenges his behavior. It is reminiscent of feudal times when the subjects waited for the queen to arrive, but not vise-a-versa. Derelict managers come late to meetings to show that they are busy. In addition, they feel their time is more precious; therefore, they cannot wait for anyone. All of this is an idiotic illusion. If a person is organized, they can arrange their time to the meeting on time—unless they think their importance doesn't allow them to wait for anyone. I used to have a boss who always came late to meetings. In the middle of meetings he took telephone calls while everyone else waited, and then declared that he had to leave early. He thought he was demonstrating to us that he was an important and very busy person. In reality, everyone thought he was rude and disorganized.

You will never hear the truth from the people who report to you.

■■■■

Regardless of how much you try to be "one of the boys" by behaving in a very friendly and informal manner, your subordinates will always be somewhat afraid of you and you will never hear the truth from them. Again, this is not fraudulent; it is another form of self-defense. This is why a true authority acts without waiting for outside approval. If you do something wrong as a supervisor, the chances are no subordinate will criticize you openly. That does not mean that you are approved. It means they are afraid to tell you that you are a failure.

Any gut or spontaneous judgment should be backed by sober analysis.

■ ■ ■ ■

Any real success is the result of a proper balance between the spontaneous and the planned. Gut feel is intuitive pattern recognition; even its origin cannot be successfully articulated. At the same time, such intuition acquires a great deal of validity when it is verified by methodical analytical process. Everything in life cannot be the result of careful planning. There are times when intuition can be trusted and acted upon. Depending upon the magnitude of the decision, I am suggesting proper analysis should also occur.

If you are a person subject to serious personal behavior shortcomings, do not seek a position of leadership.

■■■■

One should always understand the requirement for ethical behavior before they accept a position of leadership. A person that understands their shortcomings should be humble enough not to seek such a position. Again, this is a case where the requirement of the job is that the person does not fail by defacing the sovereignty of their leadership. If you know by past experience that you can be subject to lewd and inappropriate behavior, you do not become a preacher of the gospel.

After you rest, you want to get tired again.

■ ■ ■ ■

We usually express a wish for something that we don't have and it is the opposite of what we are experiencing. We should understand that this want is in relation to a present cycle and that our wishes for anything are cyclical and cannot wish for something forever. For example, if we are unhappy, we want to be happy. But we cannot appreciate happiness without having experienced the opposite. Therefore, if we are tired, we look for a state of rest. We should know this only is valid as the opposite side of the present cycle.

Loving animals and eating meat are not mutually exclusive.

■ ■ ■ ■

It is a mistake to apply moral values and attitudes that work for human beings to the rest of the universe. The commandment, "Thou shall not kill," has a limited application and experience has shown that it doesn't apply the same way everywhere. The natural way is to "eat each other," and doing so does not manifest anger or evil behavior. People who have a need to crusade develop wild ideas about the involvement of morality in the fundamental attitudes of nature. In this way we call certain animals "mean" just because they survive by eating and killing. Of course, certain animals we like. All of this is a result of over intellectualizing the process of life.

Your mind processor is the same as your muscles; if you don't use it, it atrophies.

■ ■ ■ ■

Being able to handle stress and not avoiding it makes us more expert in being able to solve any problem we may encounter. It is only when we avoid the anxiety of not knowing the future that we defeat the present. It is another case where when we're tired we look for a period of rest and we will do anything to achieve it. This is why people create a custom-made world that they live in and enjoy, because made-up concepts remove the necessity of not having an answer for everything. We should be comfortable not knowing the future and understand that we cannot put the universe in our head.

Do not look for peace of mind. The ultimate state is one of manageable anxiety.

■ ■ ■ ■

Here the words "manageable anxiety" is of importance. What I am pointing out is that the ultimate state of a human being is being able to handle problems as they arise, without being overloaded by them. Peace of mind is the result of having succeeded in overcoming some obstacle and by definition it should be a temporary situation no matter how enjoyable.

The human mind should be used to process information and one's judgment can determine how difficult the situation is that we try to solve and not try to do the impossible.

If a person is overloaded with detailed information, he or she shall daydream.

■ ■ ■ ■

We have a measurable rate of processing gases, liquids, and solids. This rate is loosely called metabolism. For example, we can measure the amount of oxygen that we process in a normal situation. If we are given too much we hyperventilate and if we're given to little, we begin to suffocate. I propose that each one of us have a definite rate of processing new bits of information which characterizes our being. If we deliver a great deal of information at a very fast rate, the person will be overloaded and will shut off the reception. They may daydream or get up and go to the bathroom. To effectively transmit worthwhile information, it has to be done at the rate which the subject can assimilate.

If you don't get involved with the music, it becomes noise.

■ ■ ■ ■

To be appreciated, music has to be listened to and followed. If it becomes the background of something that is more important, then it can become a distraction or perceived as noise. This is why music that we use for background is usually boring and has no particular character.

The sadness of winning is that the game is over.

■ ■ ■ ■

That is why the fun of winning can be thought of as an opportunity to start a new game. The fact is, games are connected and none are really detached from the others. The separation is only in our mind.

To make someone laugh you have to connect with his or her culture.

■■■■

Before telling a joke, a well-meaning person should ascertain it will be perceived as funny. What is considered humorous is not always the same because different people laugh at different things. Because we all come from different cultures, therefore, this implies that for a successful delivery, one should have previous knowledge of the culture or the audience and then act appropriately.

My ambition is to make money and be able to spend it with a happy heart.

■ ■ ■ ■

We all know that money is a means to an end. Depending on our moral system, how we acquire wealth becomes an important matter. The process of acquiring the wealth should be governed by our value system. For example, we do not plan to cheat, violate the national laws, or engage in unethical behaviors just to become rich. When the money is acquired by honest and ethical means, then one's ability to spend it is filled with the joy of real achievement. Any past regrets may tarnish that joy.

You don't dance to get to the other side of the floor.

■■■■

It is not necessary to feel that all endeavors have to acquire value during a process or at the end. The fact is, depending on the character of the endeavor, the enjoyment can be either in the journey or at the achievement of the objective. When we communicate with people for the purpose of enjoying the time we spent together, we are not likely to measure the passing time. Conversely, if we have to arrive at some end result, such as taking a trip in order to be present somewhere, then we have to concentrate on being there at the desired time.

Never have a policy that cannot be rationally defended by the executive staff.

■ ■ ■ ■

Wise management treats its subordinates as intelligent and mature people. It is on this basis that one should never have a stupid policy for the sake of having structure. All policies should make sense and they should be explained to those who have to follow them. Only in infancy are we required to do certain things and obey the authority without an accompanying rational explanation. When management expects people to obey just because "it is policy," the people are being treated as non-human beings.

Rank has less privileges.

■■■■

There is a common failing that managers exhibit when they think that just because they have a title, it justifies arbitrary and irrational behavior. The fact is, they are in a fish bowl and everyone is interested and can be critical of what they are doing and they cannot afford to fail. Again, subordinates may not tell his boss he is rude or inadequate, but they will talk behind his back and thus become destructive. You are not as free to be yourself and as unpredictable as you can be when you are the boss. It is expected that you act properly at all times and not in a way that you have to say you're sorry.

You will be remembered for doing what you don't have to do.

■ ■ ■ ■

No one will give you credit for doing your job one way or the other. But if someone feels that you have done something out of your own heart, then they will love you forever. You can give the expected bonus to the subordinate, the amount of which is determined by the structure established by the company. But if you do something in addition, such as a plaque or an inscribed crystal, with a note that you appreciate the person's performance, he will spend the money but will remember you every time he sees the crystal on the mantelpiece. One should never hesitate to be generous in occasions like this.

No matter how big you get, don't forget what you knew when you were one of the boys.

■ ■ ■ ■

One should never be dazzled by the representations of achievement, such as money, title, fame, and the like. When you feel that you have become a different person and you forget where you came from, you begin to degenerate. It is not that a person should continuously wear a veil of humility, it is rather that a person should never forget that some of those achievements have limited value.

Definitions

An invention is a new combination of old things.

■ ■ ■ ■

This is another way of stating an ancient Greek statement, that there is nothing new under the sun. The human brain can only combine in a novel manner whatever it has stored. Things that we have not experienced cannot be recognized and, therefore, cannot be used as original. When we invent something, we reprocess things that we know already and combine them in a way that could be novel in order to solve a problem.

Life is curly. Do not straighten it out.

■ ■ ■ ■

Life happens as it happens. It is not always under our control and we're not responsible for making it perfect. If you come home and your wife says, "You forgot to buy the milk," you can always answer, "you see, life is curly and my forgetting it today is equivalent to my having remembered it yesterday." Our expectations should always be in accordance with what is possible in nature. We should never expect to alter it because we have no authority in that area.

Elegance is the absence of redundancy.

■■■■

If we go to school, we store in our minds concepts and principles that have been discovered by people who lived before us. If, for example, we learn to become a civil engineer, we learn the first principles governing the bending of beams according to their length, cross-section, and material. When we graduate and we get a job, we may be required to build a bridge. If we use the acquired knowledge correctly, we will design a bridge that has the characteristic of elegance. That is: it has maximum strength and contains minimum material. If we were uneducated, and did not know any of the first principles involved, and wanted to make it strong, we would make it out of a solid concrete and an observer would call it a stupid design. This is because it contains material that is not used effectively. The design is redundant. That is the opposite of elegance.

Elegance is an optimum design.

■ ■ ■ ■

According to the previous statement, elegance is contained in an optimum design. An organization is elegant when each member works effectively and there is no wasted effort. A life is elegant if it contains almost no clutter at all. This is when we do not try to do impossible things, believe in things that don't exist, and we do things in an effortless and expert manner.

Once survival is guaranteed we get concerned about its quality.

■ ■ ■ ■

When we do not worry about survival we begin to become civilized. We are concerned about achieving a life of high quality and excellence behavior. Societies in the past that enjoyed a certain amount of security developed some very lofty ideas and philosophies that benefitted the rest of the world. They had time to think about the design of their civilization because they were busy making sure they survived any kind of adversity.

Companies degenerate when they place form above substance.

■■■■

There is no question that using the proper form deserves a lot of merit. But just being merely well-dressed, polite, and soft spoken is not enough to win the game. Excellent form should be accompanied by real substance when we have high expectations of personal achievement. We should be concerned when the enterprise we are running places extreme emphasis on form and de-emphasizes the lack of substance. Large companies make this mistake all the time. They hire people who dress well, talk well, and have excellent manners and simultaneously have no passion, perseverance, or shrewdness to over-achieve.

Government is an enterprise with captive investors.

■ ■ ■ ■

If you don't invest in my government, I put you in jail. Government usually runs in the red and if they ask for more investment we are required to oblige. It is as if they require us to all buy shares in the enterprise according to our income. This is why when the government shows a profit (surplus), it declares a dividend which obviously has to go back to those who have bought the most shares. This is why any kind of a refund usually appears to be destined to the wealthy. They are the ones who invested the most and own most of the shares that are subject to the dividend.

Typical investors are like sheep.
They follow each other.

■■■■

I do not mean to be ignominious with the above statement. However, in my experience, when I tried to raise money for companies, the usual question asked by an investor is "who else is in it?" Investors form an invisible fraternity since they like to participate in companies where their friends have already invested. They believe that this apparently reduces the risk of making a decision since they understand that other people, whom they respect, have decided to participate.

Entrepreneurs want to control situations by using their own rules. Bureaucrats want to control situations by using someone else's rules.

■ ■ ■ ■

This definition illustrates why they threaten each other. Entrepreneurs have been defined by many as demanding, difficult to manage, and rebellious employees. Bureaucrats, whose security depends on following a pre-existing structure, are threatened by anyone who suggests a change in the rules. A bureaucrat who is going from point A to point B will usually take the train because he is very willing to accept the existing structure and does not have to use his judgment during the trip. An entrepreneur will take a machete and hack a new path through the jungle because he is not interested in arriving at point B at a particular time; rather he is looking for an adventure and enjoys making decisions when there is a change in the path.

Software is a science concerned with the analytical view of the process of making a decision.

■■■■

The computer is anthropomorphic. It contains storage and a way of manipulating it in a very analogous manner in which human beings perform intelligent decisions. Software scientists study the elements that are involved in making a decision and use electronic circuits to simulate the human mind.

Nature does not behave according to any laws. Laws are human inventions that approximately describe the observed regularities.

■ ■ ■ ■

We have developed a very successful technology by digitizing nature and processing results. The result is we have invented certain relationships in the world around us. We have lost perspective that all of this is made up. Most people believe that centimeters, miles, seconds, hours and degrees of temperature, and the like truly exist. The fact is they do not and they are all a result of human imagination. Nature does not behave according to any laws in the same way that noses were not made to support spectacles. All the laws we have invented merely describe, approximately, what is going on around us. Reality is that everything is continuous and connected with each other.

Motivation is a process where I get what I want, without giving an order.

■ ■ ■ ■

In order to accomplish a result, we can force it by becoming an authoritarian and scaring people into some sort of behavior. Another way of doing, which involves less clutter, is to first understand the material we use and then set up conditions under which it will flourish naturally and produce the result we want.

Creativity is usually the result of personal stress.

■ ■ ■ ■

When companies are young with very limited resources, the players are in a stress environment in which they create themselves out of trouble and succeed. It is so amazing to me that this process is forgotten when the company succeeds and they have enough money to spend. They think that the players should not be distracted by such mundane information as the company's financial results, marketing needs, and the like. We set up luxurious laboratories where the employees can live in a peaceful atmosphere with free coffee and watermelon in the afternoon. They come to work on their bicycles, and sit around on beanbags, with the hope that they will invent something worthwhile. This atmosphere is more conducive to sleep and degeneration than creativity. In this case, people who are passionate about achieving practical results get frustrated, leave the enterprise, and form new companies.

Contempt is the killer of
any relationship.

■ ■ ■ ■

Contempt is an intriguing concept. It is a situation where one person acts in a way that decreases the self-esteem of another. It can be caused by extreme pejorative statements regarding someone's performance, or it can be the result of giving elementary instructions and treating the person like an ignoramus. I don't know of any person who relates successfully with a friend who thinks badly of them. In the face of contempt we usually leave the situation and seek a different relationship. Road rage is a manifestation of a behavior that is interpreted as contemptuous when someone cuts you off on the highway. This is why people get very upset because they think the other person does not give them the proper respect on the road.

Companies that pay attention to and glorify status symbols end up being populated by phonies.

■ ■ ■ ■

People gravitate to situations that seem to satisfy their needs. Private parking spaces, a key to the executive wash room, and luxurious offices usually attract people who put form above substance. They feel the need to be treated like royalty and thus, they detach themselves from the rest of the employees.

Language has been invented to describe reality, but some reality eludes description and some description refers to things that do not exist.

■ ■ ■ ■

Man's greatest invention is language. It is an ability to replace the world with description and communicate effectively with others. One should always understand the limits of description and not consider everything that is described as real. This applies particularly to abstractions about which most people disagree. It is as if anything that has a name actually exists in nature, which is not true. Conversely, it should be remembered that things may exist which elude description as in the case of trying to describe a complicated human experience exactly.

A phony is a person who instills very high expectation but makes certain that he or she never gets a chance to perform.

■ ■ ■ ■

There are people who profess that they are experts in certain subjects. Or, they have extraordinary capabilities in certain fields. A phony will claim this sort of expertise, but will make sure they do not participate in a situation where their statements about themselves will be challenged, I am reminded of the example of the person who says, "I am a concert violinist," but makes sure that there is no violin so he can't be challenged to prove it.

Freedom is the opportunity to do what you are supposed to do.

■ ■ ■ ■

There are people who consider freedom to be a situation where a person can do whatever he likes, regardless of the effect on the environment. This can only be done if someone lived alone in a country of no name. As soon as they develop a relationship, then freedom takes on a different meaning. The establishment of the relationship will result in certain obligations that will have to be fulfilled freely. As soon as we make an agreement, then freedom can describe our opportunity to honor it. Freedom is the leeway we have in performing according to a plan or an orchestrated manner. Freedom is exhibited by the ballerina who dances the Swan Lake ballet without violating the choreography by putting something of her own into it, which makes it particular to her performance.

Intelligence is the way we manipulate stored information.

■ ■ ■ ■

Our natural sensors pick up information from the environment, which is then coded and stored in our brain. That information can be manipulated later by establishing means of retrieving it, and developing relationships between different stored experiences. We can only manipulate the information that we have stored. People exhibit different rates of processing and memories of varying sizes.

Humility is the capacity to give proper credit to positive fortuitous influences when an over-achievement occurs.

■■■■

When the actual performance is much larger than the expected, one can call this an accident. Usually over-achievement causes most people to lose their humility and consider themselves competent rather than lucky. Since the result is commendable, they tend to want to take full credit. The converse is also true if the results exhibit under-achievement, and then, of course, they will blame it all on outside circumstances. Wisdom is synonymous to being able to understand one's role in a case of over- and under-achievement.

Enthusiasm is the positive drive resulting from de-emphasizing the negative aspects of a decision.

■ ■ ■ ■

There are times when we develop a passion for a particular direction. This passion can be called enthusiasm when it is the result of accentuating the positive aspects of the decision and thus, de-emphasizing the negative. This sometimes can lead to disaster, but, unfortunately it is a necessary ingredient for achieving the impossible.

Quantity never makes up
for lack of quality.

■ ■ ■ ■

Quality occurs when the actual performance is equal to or better than expected. It has to do with the description of the character of the behavior that determines the outcome. This can never be corrected by increasing anything such as the effort, the time, the resources, etc. If something lacks quality it has to be fixed in a fundamental way and cannot be superficially corrected by the size of investment.

Growth happens when the external authority becomes internal.

■ ■ ■ ■

When we start learning about the world around us, most commands come from an authority and we obey because we need its approval for own security. So, we go on behaving in a way that it can be approved by an outside source. This works traditionally, but we have a responsibility as we grow to internalize the principles and guidance for good personal behavior. We do good work and behave properly, not because someone ordered it, but because we understand that it "works."

Guilt is an immobilizing force.

■ ■ ■ ■

Feeling guilty can be a devastating experience that emphasizes our failure but does not inspire us to do better and maintain our self-esteem. Taking responsibility for our actions, good or bad, should encourage us to be actively pursuing excellence, rather than feeling we will not amount to anything. There is huge difference between feeling guilty and understanding we have to work to improve ourselves. The former is very negative and the latter is very constructive.

Art is when the artist is the customer. Artistic is something created for a paying customer.

■ ■ ■ ■

Most progressive and creative artists are not concerned about external approval. They have a passionate feeling that their art "should be appreciated". This is when they introduce into the world new directions and ideas in art. Sometimes they are not appreciated until they die. Conversely, if an artist creates something as a result of trying to sell the product and make a living, then we call that artistic. It may have less enduring value and may even be superficial, but it helps the artist to survive in a competitive world.

Working Hard

Never try to show diligence.
Just get involved.

■ ■ ■ ■

We are conditioned to show we are hard workers. The emphasis is on demonstrated effort and not much is said about the expected results. When we want to be diligent we declare the amount of time it took to get something done. This is because we are not involved in the process and we want to show regardless of the results, we should be approved of, because we demonstrated an interest in our work. If we get involved, we never count the time. Lovers sitting on a park bench under the moonlight became so involved with each other that they lose track of time and suddenly realize it is two o'clock in the morning and they should get home.

"I'm doing my best" is the phrase of a loser.

■ ■ ■ ■

I have never heard of a successful person say "I'm doing my best." This is a phrase that is designed to prepare the authority for a failure, at the same time seeking approval by showing diligence. "I'm doing my best" is not news. I expect it.

Trying means nothing.
Accomplishing is everything.

■ ■ ■ ■

In our earlier years when we fail at something, our parents would say, "It's okay, at least you tried". This attitude can maim our psyche to the point where we feel comfortable because we have expended effort even if the results were not achieved. In the real world, any effort expended is not really noticeable. Playing the game is for sportsmen. For real achievers, obtaining the desired results is paramount. If I am about to sky dive and I ask my assistant, "Did you pack my parachute well?" and he replies, "I tried, and I did my best", it won't be an acceptable answer if I find myself hurling to the ground in a closed chute. I don't care if he spent all day Saturday packing the chute, it must open when I pull the cord. We call it "parachute reliability" when we ask someone to achieve certain results and failure is not an option.

Working hard means you are doing something unpleasant or you are taking too long.

■ ■ ■ ■

When we are young we are told that success is the result of hard work. That is an illusion because success is the result of emphasizing the ultimate result and not the means to obtaining it. How hard one works, that is, how much time they spent at it, is not the important thing. If an employee spends too much time on a project, it costs too much and reduces the profit of the company. Working hard is mowing the lawn of a rented house or cleaning the barbeque after you have eaten the steak. This is why no one does it.

Don't take your briefcase home.
You interfere with the development
of pleasant relationships.

■ ■ ■ ■

An employee's day should be enough to accomplish any desired result. If a person is disorganized, if they are trying to do something they don't know how, or if they want to show diligence, they take their proverbial briefcase home. Don't try to impress me by showing you expend extraordinary effort. You can obtain my approval by showing that you are a professional and you can achieve the maximum in a minimum amount of time. There is no point in being driven obsessively to show diligence at the expense of a healthy and normal home life. I am excluding a crisis situation when you may actually sleep at work if it is required.

Don't tell me you are busy.
Tell me what you finished.

■ ■ ■ ■

Those who are driven by hard work, are constantly motivated to show they are eternally engaged in some sort of required activity, This is, again, a situation where the employee emphasizes effort at the expense of results. The objective of any project is to finish it, and go on to something else.

If you try hard enough you may accomplish anything, assuming you have infinite time.

■ ■ ■ ■

The thought that anything can be accomplished if one tries hard enough, is an illusion. It can only occur if a person has infinite time to expend on the effort. We are all different people with complicated and specific personalities. It is our responsibility to find the type of activity that suits us and where we can succeed with a minimum effort. This takes personal growth, getting to know one's abilities and being comfortable with this knowledge. There is no point in trying to beat oneself into an image that was suggested long ago by the authority, as it does not have any more real value.

One should achieve an intelligent perspective about money.

■■■■

If you have one hundred dollars, it makes sense to save pennies. If you have one hundred thousand dollars it makes sense to save thousands of dollars. If you have millions of dollars it makes sense to save hundreds of thousands of dollars. But if you have millions of dollars and you save pennies, you are sick. If we take seriously the symbol of a piggy bank we can be maimed for life because we become misers and lose one of the most important qualities a person could have: to be generous. Generosity does not only involve money, it involves the use of our time, talent, feeling, etc. Being generous is attractive and it is a necessary ingredient for any leader who wants to succeed. It is so discouraging to visit a very rich person's house and be served cheap champagne. One wonders why he does that? The answer is, he is sick and needs help.

Believe and apply the "effortless way". Go with nature rather than against it.

■ ■ ■ ■

The smart way of working is always determine the "grain" of the situation and going with it. It is the difference between sailing and power boating. When a person sails, he has a responsibility to use the environment to his benefit. No one argues with the wind. This idea is to posture oneself in a way that resonates with the environment and helps the ship get to the destination effortlessly. In contrast, the power boater goes against the sea, the wind, and the currents by expending lots of fuel, creating a lot of noise, and pollution. The "effortless way" requires wisdom and a wish to achieve a great result without offending anyone. Great companies have policies that are according to human nature rather than obnoxious rules that enrage everyone.

The difference between a professional and an amateur is how long it takes to finish a job.

■ ■ ■ ■

Have you ever tried to hang sheet rock or wallpaper? As an amateur you suffer, it takes a long time, and it is sheer torture…until you learn how. Knowing what to do involves removing all the clutter that is caused by choosing the wrong direction, employing the wrong principles, and repeating costly work. One can complete a project in record time by eliminating waste and unnecessary moves. Spending a lot of time to complete a project is to believe that quantity will cause quality, which is an illusion.

Don't Save Money.
Make Money.

■ ■ ■ ■

*There is no question that money is power and thus very desirable.
If most of the money you have is the result of meticulous saving,
the chances are you missed the joy of life. If you concentrate on
becoming marketable, profitable, and understand the elements of a
business person, you will persevere in making money instead, and
thus enjoy the journey.*

Being rich is having money.
Being wealthy is being able to spend it.

■ ■ ■ ■

*Money is always a means to an end. It has value when it can
be exchanged for something desirable. Too many people are
concerned about amassing a lot of money. In the process of
acquiring it, they lose the ability to enjoy the outcome. Many
destructive and abusive people have money. They try to achieve
happiness by thinking anything has a price. They don't understand
that the only thing that has a price is something for sale. Most
great things are not for sale. They have to be cultivated and,
therefore, require considerable wisdom.*

Celebrities require constant approval.

■■■■

Celebrities suffer from an over-evaluation of the importance. Most of them know the world has exaggerated their value and thus feel the need of constant approval. This is why they engage in different crusades so they can attribute to themselves additional value in order to deserve the expressed admiration.

Epilogue

Epilogue

Alan Watts once told me, "You can try with all your passion to win the game, but it really becomes worthwhile when all the effort and the wish to succeed is floated on top of an idea that it does not make any difference." He was pointing out to me in a subtle way that in our endeavor to achieve results, our state-of-mind and happiness depends on our ability to properly balance the serious versus the non-serious. We, who have been brought up under the Judeo/Christian ethic, seem to get a polarized view of the world. Things to us are either black or white, good or bad, clean or dirty, etc. We have to learn a new point of view, where all opposites are inseparable and co-exist. It is with this in mind that we can achieve a positive attitude by learning to negotiate the serious and the non-serious. I belive that most psychological troubles, such as depression and anxiety, are usually the result of taking things too seriously and truly suffering when the actual is not better than the expected.

We have to understand that we appreciate life on two levels. First we get involved in the practical life, design and obey rules to try and achieve ambitious results. To do this we have to have a reasonably serious attitude that our efforts have a definite value and they are designed to achieve excellent results. We believe that all man-made inventions such as the laws of physics, units for measuring, truly exist and we use these concepts to develop a technology that has made man king of this planet. Without losing any passion or zeal for accomplishing our goals, I invite you to consider another point of view: that we are part of a universal continuum in which things only change in form and such things as beginning and end, life and death, are mere definitions. Many religious mystics have proposed this other form of consciousness as a manifestation of personal enlightenment.

My point is that these two points co-exist. They do not oppose each other. We should not prefer one over the other. We should understand that the individual and personal point of view can co-exist with the universal one in a way that we achieve an optimum idea of what is going on. This is a very hard thing to do. Most of us are seeking one answer, which is not enough. Most of us want to know, "What is it all about?' as if there is an answer. Alan Watts would have called this an inappropriate question. Seek an appropriate balance between the two apparently different points of view, understanding that they are both correct.

If we learn to do that, and it requires a great deal of introspection, we may not make money or become famous, but it can remove the "panic" from our life. It is not that we become more detached or consider things in a more optimistic or light-hearted way. Instead, we are able to understand the relationship between serious and non-serious. This will be particularly helpful when the actual is less than expected, in which case instead of feeling guilty, incompetent, and less valuable, we are encouraged to exercise action to correct the situation and satisfy our expectations once more. We also learn to examine our expectations for validity and eliminate all those that are the result of our early upbringing which may be impossible or anachronistic. That is what "personal growth" is all about.

When we grow up we develop this ability to change our point of view, modify our expectations, and thus, come closer to the truth and to a realistic point of view about life.

Renn Zaphiropoulos

Renn Zaphiropoulos

Renn Zaphiropoulos holds a BS in Engineering Physics and a MS in Physics from Lehigh University, Bethlehem, Pennsylvania. He was awarded an Honory Doctorate of Engineering from the Rose-Hulman Institute of Technology in Terre Haute, Indiana, as well as an Honorary Doctorate of Business and an Honorary Doctorate of Humanities from Southern Utah University, Cedar City, Utah.

He has 29 patents and many publications to his credit. He retired as a Corporate Vice President from the Xerox Corporation in 1988. He is a frequent lecturer on management subjects and serves on the board of directors of several high-tech companies. He also conducts seminars, executive training, and is a consultant to several top management executives.

This material may not be reproduced without written permission by the author

For additional information contact:
Renn Zaphiropoulos
PO Box 1022
12500 West Highway 56
Cedar City, UT 84720

Home number: 435.586.5922
Fax number: 435.865.1000
E-mail address: Zaph@inxsnet.com